BLAIRSVILLE-SALTSBURG
SCHOOL DISTRICT
Date_____ No._____

Linda Bennett (when she was 17 years old) from Medicine Hat, Alberta, Canada, surrounded by some of her trophies. She was city champion for seven years.

BATON TWIRLING

BY NANCY L. ROBISON

Harvey House · New York

The author wishes to thank the following for their help and assistance in writing this book:
Bill Whitehead for photo assistance
Karen Matossian
Jacqueline McGrory
California Twirling Corps Association
National Twirling Corps Association
Santa Barbara Twirlers
San Gabriel Twirlers
Temple City Twirlers
Monteclair Twirlers
Anaheim Twirlers.

Copyright © 1980 by Nancy L. Robison

All rights reserved, including the right to
reproduce this book or portions thereof in any form.

Manufactured in the United States of America

ISBN 0-8178-5999-3
Library of Congress Card Catalog No. 78-73746

Harvey House, Publishers
20 Waterside Plaza, New York, N.Y. 10010

Published in Canada by Fitzhenry & Whiteside, Ltd., Toronto

TABLE OF CONTENTS

History 9

Types of Batons 15

Learning to Twirl 25

Fun with your Baton 45

CHAPTER ONE • HISTORY

The first baton was not for twirling at all and the baton would go through many changes before it was. Originally a long stick, the baton was used by a conductor of an orchestra, band or chorus to keep tempo and beat while the group played or sang. In the year 1600, the baton was a long rod which was struck on the floor in time with the music. Today, a conductor holds a short thin stick in his hand and waves it to direct a musical group.

The conductor's long baton led to the drum major's marching band and eventually to the elaborate baton twirlers we expect to see perform in parades and pageants.

During the "Band Craze" era in the late 1800s — when there were over 10,000 military bands in the United States alone — people became accostumed to seeing a drum major in charge of keeping the strong beat of the music. It is possible that these drum major soon became performers, as well as musical conductors. Perhaps to entertain the listening audience, the drum majors began to twirl and throw their batons into the air. It is hard to determine exactly when the baton twirler — concerned with solely performing and **not** with leading a musical group — got into the act but some say it began with the Swiss Flag Swingers.

Swiss Flag Swingers originated in the Alps where the people used flags to send messages over great distances from mountain top to mountain top. Later on, the brightly colored flags were used to lead parades and were displayed at all festivals. In parades the Swiss banner carrier takes the lead and as he marches, pitches his flag high into the air and catches it again. As the flag swinger marches, he twirls his flag to the music using either both hands or just one. He passes the flag between his legs, around his body and into the air similar to baton twirling. With the flag removed, leaving just the metal bar, a much easier instrument remains to maneuver around the body and to twirl in the many varieties of movements we see today.

Baton twirling competitions may have been patterned after the Swiss. In Swiss Flag Swinging competition, tricks are often improvised to produce new effects. A variety of twirls are adapted to give style and freshness to the basic moves. Baton twirling competitions work this way too. Twirlers dance to jazz music or rhythmic beats while at the same time tossing their batons high in the air, or to one another, or whirling it around their bodies and in and out of their legs. Acrobatics and tumbling are sometimes added to give yet another dimension to the routine.

Another theory is that baton twirling originated with the Hawaiians who twirl flaming torches and sticks. With two hands, they spin their torches or sticks under the legs and around their bodies while dancing to the fast beat of drums.

Baton twirling could also have developed from the Samoan Sword Spinners. Originally part of a religious ceremony, the sword spinners pretended to duel with their swords until one conquered the other. The winner captured the loser's sword and hooked it together with his own and then twirled it over his head in triumph.

Like the Swiss custom, sword spinning is an art passed down from generation to generation. Samoan Sword Spinning has all the motions of baton twirling and might easily have influenced modern baton twirling in North America.

Years ago, the minstrel dancers of the South used canes to dance with and they often twirled the cane through their fingers as part of dance routines. This too could have been a spark toward the baton twirler of today.

In the early 1930s, the drum majorette's skill and ability to lead a parade and to twirl the metal bar was considered very special. Since that time, the art and skill of baton twirling has spread across the United States and is finding some interest in foreign lands as well.

What makes this sport so fascinating to so many?

1.) Baton twirling can be performed by people of all ages, from tiny tots to adults. 2.) It is enjoyed by both girls and boys, men and women. In fact, Calvin Murphy, a professional basketball player for the Houston Rockets, practices baton twirling to keep himself in shape for the basketball season. He's even twirled in competition and during halftimes at football games. 3.) Baton twirlers find freedom and expression in inventing original routines. 4.) Having a chance to win trophies and recognition at competitions can be a thrill.

Baton twirling has grown over the past 170 years from more than just leading a band parade to a fulltime sport enjoyed by millions. Today it provides entertainment at sporting events, is sometimes used on television to advertise products and is enjoyed by those who just like being involved in a sport they can do.

At a recent national championship meet, more than 5,000 young contestants showed up. They performed in front of judges, demonstrating their strength and original routines. Some had developed new tricks, using leaps and jumps and gymnastic stunts. Musical routines varied from jazz to blues, and tricks ranged into the realm of the impossible.

No one is quite sure how baton twirling all began; but wherever it came from, it's here now and enjoyed by many.

CHAPTER TWO • TYPES OF BATONS

Batons come in different lengths — usually in an even number of inches — and descriptions. Your choice of baton will depend on whether you are a drum major leading a band or a majorette strutting out in front of a parade.

A drum major requires a very long staff to allow the last row members of a band to see his lead. The staff must be held high over the head so all can see. The knob or ball on the drum major's baton is larger than on the majorette's twirling baton. The knob acts as a good-sized handle for the drum major to hold onto while whirling the staff over the head. (The masculine pronoun has been used in this description since drum majors are usually male. But, as with many jobs in our society, this is changing as well. Many girls are now drum majors.) With the staff, the drum major leads the parade, keeping the band together in rhythm, timing and pace.

Twirlers' batons have changed over the years from a heavy metal bar to a very lightweight one made of a special steel alloy. The shift of the baton has decreased in size from an inch or more in diameter to today's baton of approximately ¾-of-an-inch or smaller.

The thin shafts of modern batons have many advantages over the heavy, thicker batons of yesterday. They are easier to handle. They are lighter in weight, saving the twirlers' arms from tiring as quickly.

A baton must be properly weighted and balanced to fit the twirler. There is a proper length for everyone — unlike during the 1930s when batons came only in sizes "short," "medium," or "long." Now they are measured from the twirler's armpit to the tip of the middle finger when the arm is outstreched. A little shorter measurement is used for beginners while a little longer baton is used by more experienced twirlers. Batons may be purchased through a sales catalog, from a teacher or from almost any music store.

Several years back, batons were not as well-balanced as they are today. The head was often much too heavy which threw the balance off. The twirler had to hold the baton close to the head for better balance and in doing so gave an awkward appearance.

Earlier baton heads were often made of wood. When twirled and a mistake made, a clop on the elbow really hurt.

For all practical uses, today's batons have small heads usually made of rubber with the center of balance just slightly off center toward the head, giving the baton just enough weight to gather momentum.

Besides being used to lead parades, batons are also used for entertainment when twirlers present fancy routines. This type of twirling includes dancing, gymnastics and sometimes twirling two batons at once.

A baton that gets special attention and is used for nighttime entertainment is the fire baton. Usually this baton has a wick made of wrapped cloth on each end of the shaft. This is dipped into white gas and lit. Sometimes lighter fluid or torch fluid is used to light these wicks, but with white gas there is less smoke. Some fire batons have tiny holes in the staff to catch any excess gas that may have spilled. If a baton does not have these holes, the staff must be wiped clean before use. When using one of these, **EXTREME CAUTION** should be followed as they can be very dangerous.

A flaming baton when twirled around the body could lead to trouble if not done properly. When using the instrument in this way it is advisable to have someone standing near to take the baton and snuff out the fire. This is done by simply cupping the wicks with a soup can or by just blowing out the flame as you would a candle. These light wicks burn for only about ten minutes and will eventually burn out on their own.

Anyone standing close while a fire baton is being twirled should be informed that it uses flammable material and that they should move back. Because of the danger of fire, clothing should be kept free from fringes or any loose trim that might easily catch fire. (It is a good idea to wear a fire-proofed costume.) Also, hair should be styled close to the head. Before beginning, the twirler should check for wind and if it is windy, do **not** light the baton.

If fire is too hazardous, a specially designed battery-operated flashlight baton can be used. Colored plastic may also be inserted over each end of the flashlight to give off colored lights. The problem of using these batons is that when dropped they either break or the lights go out.

Another fun show-type baton is the ribbon baton. Using a standard baton, colored ribbons are tied on each end. This makes an interesting effect when whirled around.

CHAPTER THREE • WHAT TO KNOW BEFORE STARTING

CLOTHING AND ACCESSORIES

Clothing is an important consideration in baton twirling, not only for show but for practicality. Any outfit with fluffy, full sleeves is going to cause trouble for the baton twirler. Usually a close fitting garment is best.

At one time, majorettes wore only the "military look," complete with boots and tassels, top hat and military brass buttons and braid. Although some drum majors and majorettes carry on this tradition, majorettes have now found a way to express their individuality in their appearance. Some prefer a short skimpy jumpsuit made of glittery fabric while others wear more conservative outfits.

Groups of majorettes marching with a band usually wear costumes which match those worn by the musicians. Everything from Aztec Indians to Scottish Highlanders are represented in these groups. However, for the beginner, clothing should be comfortable and not bulky. Shorts and leotards or long pants are recommended when high kicks and leg raises are a part of the practice.

Long hair should be tied back for safety reasons. When whirling the baton around you don't want to get it tangled up in flowing hair. And if hats or other headdresses are worn, they should be securely fastened so they won't slip or fall off.

Comfortable shoes are a must. Tennis shoes are not only used for practice but are preferred by many majorettes for performing. They are soft, comfortable, lightweight and easy to walk in.

MAINTENANCE

As in every other sport, good equipment is important in twirling and taking care of it is also important. Keeping shoes clean and polished is essential. When in competition, points may be subtracted for any scuff marks.

For the baton, the rubber tips can be washed with warm soapy water to keep clean. The tip and ball of the baton are usually white and are easily soiled. To prevent stains while practicing, a piece of plastic can be wrapped around each end of the baton and held on by rubber bands. If the white parts do get stained, a household cleansing powder will clean it. When cleaning the ball and tip, it is not advisable to remove them since too much handling will stretch them and then they will not fit properly. It would be embarrassing to have them fly off during a twirling routine.

The shaft of the baton can be kept sparkling clean and shiny by simply wiping it with a cloth or occasionally rubbing it down with silver polish. To prevent scratches and dents, a carrying bag can be made or purchased to store the baton.

In caring for your baton it is not wise to leave it where it can be sat on, run over or bent. Have a special safe plce to keep it in an upright position.

For easy identification it is a good idea to mark your baton in a special way. When you are with hundreds of others in a contest — and many have the same type of baton — it is easy to get equipment mixed up. So make a small mark — one that your audience cannot see — but one that you can find. Perhaps a strip of colored or plain tape with your name on it, or a nail polish mark somewhere would do.

BEING IN SHAPE

Exercise and posture are very important aspects of baton twirling. Remember you will be on your feet a lot while walking long distances, marching for miles or dancing in front of judges. The Rose Bowl Parade, held each New Year's Day in Pasadena, California, is attended by thousands of participants. The parade extends for five miles from start to finish. For this Grand Daddy of all parades, majorettes must be in good physical condition, including their feet. If they aren't ready for it, they can't do all the fancy strutting, dancing, spinning and marching that's required.

Karen Matossian stretches her legs, arms and back. In a sitting position with one leg outstretched, the other curled back, Karen reaches for her toes and tries to touch her forehead to her knee.

Side kicks with knees straight help limber the legs. Karen starts with five kicks of each leg.

Leaning back as far as she can go helps to limber up the back, neck and stomach muscles.

Karen bends from the waist and touches the ground. She does this exercise five to ten times to limber up the legs, back and arms.

High kicks are good for stretching the legs. Like side kicks, they should be done at least five to ten times for each leg.

To loosen back and side muscles, Karen twists her waist, arms and back. With the body facing forward, she moves the upper half of her body by swinging her arms right across her front, then switching and swinging left as far as she can swing across the front of her body. Repeat this motion, twisting back and forth several times.

Side leg stretches: with her weight on one leg, bend and stoop down stretching the other leg out to the side. Then change and do the stretch with the other leg.

Waist bends: arms over head, Karen bends and stretches right and left, then repeats to the other direction.

Remember to exercise slowly and do a little each day. It is better than trying to do too much at one time. Baton twirling requires strength in the back and arms, as well as tight stomach muscles. As important as good exercise is good posture.

Part of good posture is a straight back with your head held high. Body position must be correct at all times. Shoulders hunched over look awkward and out of balance. Keep toes pointed or leg work will look sloppy. Knees stiff when standing will look better than loose sagging knees that give you an off-balance appearance.

With practice, good posture comes easily and automatically. All stiffness will dissolve into a smooth natural appearance and rhythm. Music is added to help keep your march or strut in time. But before starting, be sure you have sufficiently exercised and that your posture is correct.

SCHOOLS

There are baton twirling classes in most cities which are often taught by former baton twirling champions or dance teachers.

In these special schools, you not only learn how to twirl a baton, but how to enter contests as well as how to march with a band. In some schools you will be taught how to put a dance routine together whether for contests or entertainment purposes.

Many parts and recreation departments give baton instructions, as do some youth organizations. But, going to a baton twirling school will help you learn more quickly under the experienced eye of a teacher. Also, you will meet and make friends with others who are interested in the sport, making it more fun.

CHAPTER FOUR • LEARNING TO TWIRL

Learning to twirl can be both fun and interesting if you don't let yourself get discouraged. When learning, it is a good idea to use a shorter baton than is suggested for your arm length. A shorter baton will be easier for you to handle and is more comfortable.

MARCHING

Now that we are ready to begin, marching may be a good place to start.

Although the accent is on wrist action, in baton twirling the rest of the body must be coordinated in order to have a smooth and rhythmic look.

First, check your posture. Are your head and chin up? Are your shoulders back, weight balanced evenly on both feet, legs together, toes straight ahead? With the baton held lightly between the first two fingers and down at your side, you should stand tall and straight and begin to mark time in place. Right, left, right, left.

When your arm finally gets tired, rest and practice walking or marching around the yard with knees up high, toes pointed down. March on the balls of your feet.

Knees are up and toes are down. When ready to go, you march forward ... toe-heel, toe-heel (not heel-toe). Then with a natural swing and in time to the music you are on your own way.

A professional teacher can help you with routines and fundamentals of baton twirling but only **you** can put it to work. Confidence plays an important part. Sometimes you will make a mistake, but that is the time to keep going. To pause and sulk over your mistake will make your performance worse, but to continue on and pick up where you left off can only help you improve. Even if you don't feel confident, you can look it. You will be surprised how much this will help you keep going during a performance.

Nervousness will sometimes make the knees weak and the palms sweaty. There are not many known remedies for weak knees in times of stress and pressure, but limbering up, doing deep knee bends and stretching exercises will help. Sweaty palms can be cured by pressing the hands on a handkerchief with corn starch powder tied inside.

IT'S ALL IN THE WRIST

Baton twirling is done with wrist action. A limber wrist is most essential. Without a free moving wrist, you may find the baton slapping your elbow pretty hard. Grasping the baton too tightly will prevent a relaxed spin, so keep your grip loose. Change hands often to learn both right and left movements and at the same time give your arms a rest. If it feels awkward, don't worry. Soon your muscles will develop and you will become stronger. Sometimes it is helpful to put the hand not in use on the hip, thereby getting it out of the way. Also, practice smiling while twirling the baton and keeping your feet close together. Enjoy it and practice, practice, practice.

For the most basic one-handed twirl, the baton is held in the middle of the shaft with the palm down. Variations of hand positions are explained with each trick.

TWIRLS

In the following twirls you will note there are several variations to the basic twirl. Different arm motions and placements make the difference. But to learn the basics is the first step, then the variations will fall nicely into place.

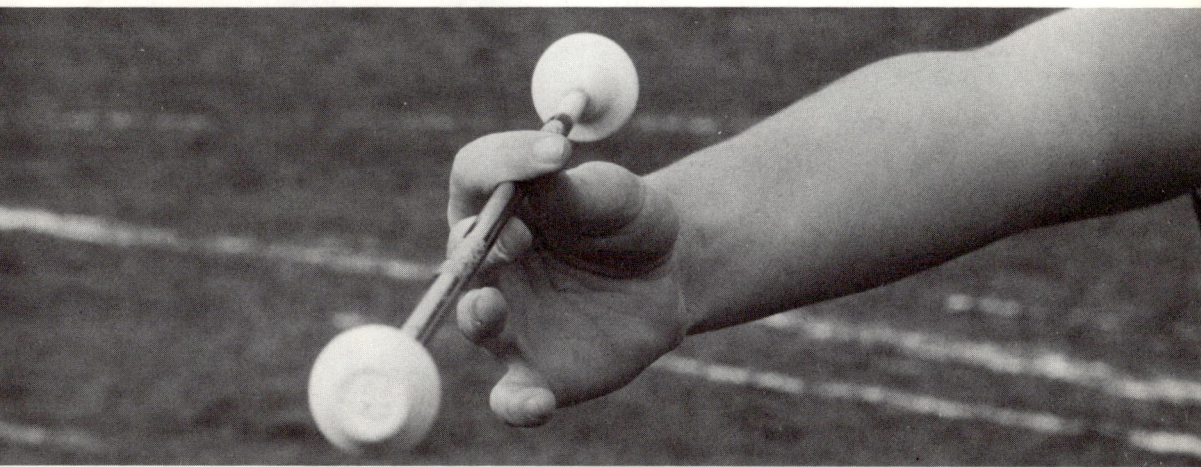

With her wrist relaxed, Jacqueline McGrory demonstrates the proper way to hold the baton for beginning an exercise. The baton is held mostly with the thumb and forefinger.

BASIC TWIRL

Over the years, twirls have changed in name. For instance: SIDE CIRCLES have also been called PANCAKE TWIRLS or HORIZONTAL SPINS. CARTWHEELS are also known as THE BUTTERFLY or WINDMILL. Whatever the name, the twirl has remained basically the same. Here are some to start you off. They are fairly easy to do.

Pancake or Horizontal Twirl

Extend your arm out to the side and hold the staff in the center with the head facing away from you. Move the baton forward with the head passing over the top of your arm, the tip will be on the bottom. Turn your wrist around, weaving the baton over your arm and under your arm. Over, under. Now twirl faster until you feel comfortable. Then try it with the other hand. Shift from one hand to the other in one motion without stopping the twirl. Try it.

Jacqueline prepares to twirl the pancake. With her arm out to the side, she holds the staff in the center and the ball facing away from her.

She moves the ball forward, using her fingers to push the staff around. As the ball comes forward, it will pass over the top of her arm and the tip will pass under her arm.

After she practices with the right arm, she shifts to the left and repeats the same maneuvers.

PANCAKE DOWN or CIRCLE DOWN or WRIST TWIRL

The difference between this twirl and the Pancake Twirl is that now the baton is down at your side and the head goes inside next to your body and the tip goes outside passing your elbow. (Watch out for your elbow. Don't bang it.) Keep your arm straight and you won't hit yourself.

With the wrist relaxed, hold the baton mostly with the thumb and first finger. The baton is held loosely in the hand with the ball or head pointing forward. The other fingers touch the shaft lightly and help push the baton around. By turning the wrist forward the head will swing around in a complete circle on the inside of the arm, next to the body. The tip of the baton rotates on the outside of the arm. The elbow is not held still in this exercise but bends with the movement.

The Wrist Twirl may be done with either hand or with a baton in each hand at the same time. And it can be moved above the head or held out at the shoulder height.

She now brings the baton down to her side for the pancake down or the Circle Down twirl. This is done the same way as the pancake twirl only down at the side. This time the ball passes on the inside, next to the body and the tip goes outside next to the elbow.

Over the head Pancake Twirl. The baton is held in the center of the shaft over the head.

A swing forward with the ball leading...

The ball leads on the inside of the arm, the tip turns on the outside next to the elbow.

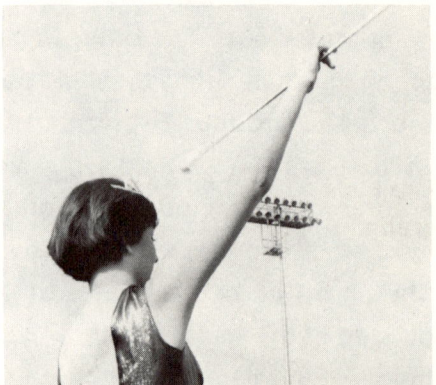

The baton comes around to almost the starting position again.

...And then it is ready to turn around again.

HAND ROLL

The Hand Roll is a variation of the Wrist Twirl. With the shaft held in the center, begin with the head pointing up toward the sky, then bring the head down facing the ground and flip the tip end over the back of the hand. In a quick motion, turn the hand around, palm up and catch the baton and repeat the exercise. This is a roll and grab spin and works well when the baton is kept centered.

The Hand Roll begins by grabbing the baton in the center and letting it roll over the back of the hand.

The Hand Roll is quick action. A grab and roll movement.

From the Hand Roll comes the Wrist Flip. Same as the grab and roll only this time the baton is flipped slightly into the air.

FISH TAIL

Begin the Fish Tail in much the same way as the Hand Roll, but instead of a grab and roll motion, leave the baton to balance on the back of the hand as you make a fish tail type of movement with your hand. The baton will balance on the back of your hand and appear to be going around your wrist. You can move your arm while your hand is fish tailing, up over your head and around to the side.

The baton is rolled on the back of the wrist while the hand moves in a swirling pattern to make a Fishtail Spin. (Whitehead photos)

FIGURE EIGHT

The Figure Eight is just like its name. The baton simply draws a figure eight across the front of the body. Hold the baton the same as for the Wrist Twirl only in front of the body instead of at the side. The head leads down in a deep arc from right to left, then it swings high across and in front of the left shoulder. Now the wrist turns over and the head or ball leads down in another long arc across the front of the body, down and away on the right side. Turning the wrist over, the head comes back up to the starting position, then falls again across the body on the far left side and the exercise is repeated again. Practice this using both hands.

To begin the Figure Eight, hold the baton in the center of the shaft. Karen lets the ball lead down across the front.

Turning the baton, she brings it back up in front and across her leading with the head up, wrist bent.

She brings the baton down, pointing with the head away from her.

With the wrist back as far as it will go...

...she brings the head up again and then...

...down across her front again.

The Figure Eight can also be twirled over the head or down at the side.

BUTTERFLY or CARTWHEEL or WINDMILL

This is like the Figure Eight only it is done at the side and over the head. Hold the baton in the center of the shaft with the right hand. With a forward wrist motion turn palm up and bring the tip toward your hip, keeping the palm up. Then turn the wrist to the right and raise the arm high above the head with the palm up. The head now points toward the back of you while the tip points toward the front and straight up. With a sweeping motion bring the arm down to the right side and turn the palm down. The tip now twirls to point toward the floor. The head end is up. Remember: Tip in. Tip out. Arm up. Arm down.

The Windmill starts at the side and winds up over the head.

With forward wrist motion, Karen brings baton up, tip pointing toward her hip.

Palm up, she raises the baton. From here she will point the head toward her back then bring it forward with a sweeping motion, leading with the tip. The ball end is up.

TWO-HAND SPIN

Most important of all twirls is the Two-Hand Spin. It is a very basic twirl and acts as a break and leads into other more complicated tricks. Hold the baton in the right hand, palm down, head pointing left. The left hand crosses over the right hand, palm up but out of the way. The wrists make an **X**. Turn the right wrist to the right all the way until the baton is ready to roll off the right thumb. The head now points to the left. The left hand comes forward, palm up, over the right hand and takes the baton turning it around so the ball is pointing to the right. The left hand turns palm down and the right hand is brought back and takes the baton to start the exercise over again. The baton turns one complete revolution in the right hand. While in the left hand it turns only one half-revolution. By continuous repetition, the baton spins in front of the body like a circle.

The Two-Hand Twirl. Both hands hold the baton in the center . . .

. . . The right hand grips the shaft and turns it while the left hand crosses over the top.

The left hand forms an X and takes the baton, palm up.

The left hand turns the baton back around to starting position with both hands on the shaft and palms down.

PASS AROUND BACK

Following the Two-Hand Spin, it is easy to pass the baton around the back. Start with the Two-Hand Spin. When the baton is in the left hand, the palm is turned down and around until the tip end makes one complete revoluton. The right hand moves around your back while the left hand carries the baton around your back to meet the right hand. The right hand takes the baton behind your back, palm up and brings it around in front of the body where it is in the correct position to start the Two-Hand Spin again.

When twirling behind the back, Jacqueline starts the Two-Hand Twirl, then grasps the baton with her left hand and swings it behind her.

Both hands are on the baton around in back.

With her right hand, she takes the baton from the left hand and brings it around in front again.

From the Two-Hand Twirl, it is easy to wrap the baton around the neck. Using the right hand, hold the baton on one end and swing it around your neck on the left side.

Baton wraps all the way around the neck and is taken by the left hand.

Arms crossed, take the baton with the left hand from around the right side and now you're ready to go again.

UNDER THE LEGS

Twirl with two-hands then take the baton in the right hand with the head pointing to the left. Lift the right leg either in a high kick or with a bent knee and toes pointing down. Bring the baton around and pass it under the leg, tip first. The left hand, palm up, grasps the baton and gives the shaft a complete turn, one full turn and passes it back to the right hand.

For passing the baton under the legs, Jacqueline starts with the Two-Hand Twirl, then grasps the end with her hand and flips it under her leg.

Sometimes it is an interesting stunt to flip the baton under the leg and then into the air.

FINGER TWIRLS

Finger Twirls may be performed by using three, four or five fingers. Your routine and the timing of the music will determine which one of these twirls to use. The three finger twirl is the easiest but at times all five fingers will be needed to make the routine come out right. Finger Twirls differ as much as the names for tricks. Maybe you can make up your own. In the meantime, here are a few finger twirls.

THREE FINGER TWIRL

Hold the baton like a pencil. Roll the baton across the first finger and then over the third finger then over the last two fingers which are held together. Palm is up. Now turn your wrist over, palm pointing down, the baton is held between the third and fourth fingers by the last two fingers. The wrist now twists back and the baton head is pointing toward the ground. With a quick wrist twist, bring the head of the baton back up facing toward you and roll the baton back through the fingers the other way. You are in the starting position again.

The Three-Finger twirl starts with the basic baton position. Karen holds it with thumb and first finger.

The baton rolls from the thumb and first finger . . .

. . . over the middle finger. All other fingers are kept back out of the way . . . .

... From the middle finger, baton is rolled over the last two fingers. ...

... Held now by the last two fingers, she turns her wrist over and ...

... starts the baton rolling back through the fingers the other way.

The baton is back to the starting position again.

The Three Finger Twirl may also be performed by rolling the baton over the first finger and then holding the second and third fingers together, roll it over them and onto the fourth finger or little finger. From the little finger, flip the baton in the air and after it has turned completely over, catch it with the first finger and you are ready to roll the baton through the fingers again.

(This twirl is a little more advanced and takes a lot of practice but once you get the rhythm it will be fun and easy.) Before starting any of the finger twirls be sure to loosen your fingers first. While in the learning process, use the left hand to guide the baton through the fingers. It is a little easier until you can feel it working. Repeat the exercise over and over until the trick becomes smooth and easy.

AERIAL WORK

Throws and catches may be made from the Finger Twirls or from the Two-Hand Twirls or almost any of the other twirls. An easy throw can be learned out of the Two-Hand Spin. Start with the head pointing left and do a Two-Hand Spin.

The Aerial Toss takes practice. Spinning the baton with both hands, it is easy to give the baton a little extra boost into the air. It will turn several times before coming down.

Now when the baton rolls off the right thumb, before catching it with the left, raise the right hand and the baton will spin off the thumb into the air. Practice throwing a few times and just letting the baton drop to the ground before trying to catch it.

Watch the center of the baton for easier catching. The outside spins but the center remains in clear vision.

Mistakes are made when the twirler takes her eyes off the baton.

To catch the toss, use the right hand, palm up and out ready to grab it. Keep your eyes on the center of the spinning baton. This is where the baton is caught. The outside of the spin will be a blur but the center will stay in clear vision. Grasp the falling baton at the center.

Believe it or not, a fast spinning baton is easier to catch than a slow moving one.

SALUTE

The Salute is a very important part of baton twirling. It is used many times; when the National Anthem is played, when beginning or ending a routine, or in a contest or exhibition and before accepting an award. There are many different salutes and some you may want to make up yourself, but it is basically standing respectfully at attention with your baton held up or down. Many times at competitions, trophies will not be awarded until some kind of salute is presented. It may be a deep bow from the waist, or an elaborate twirling routine ending in a crisp pose.

When not performing, the baton should be held at the carry position. Right arm extended forward, elbow slightly bent, hand held at belt level and palm up. The baton is rested on the forearm, tip extended past the elbow.

The Salute is used when accepting an award, when finishing a routine or when holding a pose.

STRUTS

Keep time with the cadence. Become skilled at marching. Don't sway your back. Hold your shoulders firmly back and straight. Do not touch the opposite knee with your toe as you bring the leg up. Bring the toe not more than knee height. Do not plow your foot down, place it down gently and gracefully — toe first. Don't slap the heel on the floor. Don't let your chin tilt too high in the sky and push your head back. Don't let your stomach protrude. Tuck it in and the seater too. In competition you are judged on your strutting ability so it must be smooth, rhythmic and graceful.

MARCHING ELIMINATIONS

At some meets, marching eliminations contests are held at the end of the twirling competitions. Anyone can enter. Lining up in a straight line, three or four deep and in good posture, with eyes forward, the contestants wait for the commands.

"Right turn march! Left turn march!"

Batons need not be carried at this time. Quick reactions and listening are what count here. Faster and faster the calls are made until someone misses and is dropped out of the lineup. This takes a lot of concentration as the calls get faster and more complicated. Sometimes trophies are awarded to the first, second and third place winners so it is worthwhile practicing.

These are only a few of the basic twirls but remember when you practice twirling, make your routine look restful but impressive. Never forget the basics. Avoid bent elbows, poor posture and keep smiling!

CHAPTER FIVE • FUN WITH YOUR BATON

MEETS

You can have fun twirling your baton on your own; but contests, conventions and competitions add to the interest. At these events, twirlers make new friends with co-competitors from other places. Here, they also exchange ideas on tricks and routines and it is an opportunity to see how you compare with others in competition, where your weaknesses are and where improvement is needed.

You do not need to be a member of a baton school to enter a contest. Competitive categories range from beginner to experienced and advanced twirler.

Each spring, national meets are held in different parts of the United States. Competitors are judged and graded on their ability to strut in a smooth manner while at the same time maintaining grace and rhythm. All participants have equal chances since everyone is divided into specific age and experience levels. Judges are not associated with baton schools but represent a non-biased group as a rule. There is usually a small fee charged for entering each event.

RULES, POINTS AND CLASSIFICATIONS

A point system is used with first, second and third place trophies given. Breaking down the judging, points are given for: 1.) Technique, 2.) Originality, 3.) Appearance, 4.) Style, 5.) Strut, 6.) Speed, and 7.) Presentation.

As an example in how a contest is structured, in February 1979, the California State Championships sponsored by the California Twirling Corps Association were held in Pasadena, California. There were two groups. The younger twirlers up to age fourteen formed the first group while fifteen to eighteen year olds formed the second group. Competition began at nine o'clock on Saturday morning and continued through the day until four in the afternoon. Then it was repeated the next day for the older competitors.

INSPECTION

Inspection time is the first round of competition. Groups of twirlers must stand at attention: shoulders back, legs straight, eyes forward. Everyone in the group must be in uniform or points are deducted. Hair style is agreed upon ahead of time, as is whether or not to wear make-up or headdresses. Hair dangling out of place is a point off. Bobby pins or clips showing is a point off. Eyes should focus on the inspector instead of looking straight ahead. Poor posture will take off a point. Lining up wrong will subtract a point, as will moving during the inspection. And of course being late for the inspection line will subtract a big three points. Being prompt is most important. Dirt on the baton ball or tip is a point off. All in all, inspection takes about five minutes for each group and that means standing absolutely still during that time. The inspectors, obviously, are quite picky!

(Left) Groups of twirlers stand at attention, shoulders back, legs straight, eyes forward. Everyone in the group must be in uniform for inspection. (Right) Participants must agree on hair style and whether to wear hair bows or not.

PARADE MARCH

After the inspection, each team breaks off into their groups for judging while marching on parade. Again, they are judged on neatness, appearance as a group, rhythm, difficulty of routine and how well they perform.

Beginning with the Tiny Tot Parade Teams bearing such names as **Sharp Steppers, Deb Stars, Baby Dolls** and **Rockettes,** they step out in time to pre-recorded music and twirl as they march past the judges' table.

The Tiny Tots have a shorter distance to march than do the older groups.

Now they are judged on how well they stay in step and line, how many times they drop their batons and where the leader stands and how well the group follow their leader.

Sometimes scores come out very close and are won on only a **tenth** of a point. Usually five to seven judges are selected to keep score. Each one uses separate tally sheets and then all sheets are added together for the final score of each group. On the score sheet the number 200 is given as a possible perfect score. From that is subtracted the number of errors to give a final net score.

The Tiny Tots are followed by the Juvenile Team divisions, then the Junior Parade Teams, followed by the Juvenile Parade Corps and finally the Junior Parade Corps. After the parade competition, there is a lunch break followed by the trick contests usually held in an indoor gym.

Juvenile Team divisions follow the Tiny Tots ...

Junior Parade Teams follow the Juvenile Team divisions ...

The Juvenile Parade Corps are next ...

... followed by the Junior Parade Corps.

TRICK CONTESTS

Trick contests can be performed by individuals or groups. These tricks are performed to music that has been pre-recorded except for the Field Corp Groups who are accompanied by a percussion team of drums and sometimes a cymbal that follows behind the twirlers providing them with a marching beat.

Twirlers may be judged on such items as wrist moves, finger work, leg work. They will be judged on how well they perform aerials and exchanges (tossing their batons in the air and catching them, or they will toss their batons to each other while catching the other baton in an exchange.)

Ambidexterity is another thing the judges look for. Judging on how well the twirler uses both hands, the difficulty of the routine along with the balance of the performance, number of repeated twirls and continuity are judged as well.

The Percussion Group can be seen behind the twirlers.

Twirlers exchange batons to one another by tossing them in the air while still marching.

When working with a group, the leader is evaluated on a separate sheet. She will get a circle for a superior performance or a check where improvement is needed under the following categories:

1.) Does the leader show control of her group at all times? 2.) Does she command well by whistle or by voice? 3.) Is her rhythm and timing good? 4.) Does she smile and show a lot of spirit? 5.) How is her footwork? Is she smooth? Does she march well? Does she stay in position? 6.) How does the audience react to the performance? How does the leader react to the audience? Does she have eye contact, poise and confidence? 7.) Does she carry herself well? 8.) What is the overall impression she makes?

The total possible points a leader can accumulate here are 100 points. One point is subtracted for a drop of the baton and two points for being out of step.

The overall group must perform well in these categories, too. They are also judged on their presentation. 1.) Do they follow directions? 2.) Do they maneuver well while twirling? 3.) How is their salute? 4.) Are they well spaced? 5.) Do they stay together as a team? 6.) Is their baton pattern executed well? 7.) Do they show confidence and express a pleasing personality? 8.) Are they in time with one another? 9.) Are hand changes consistent or are all the twirls done with one hand? 10.) Do they show good posture? Do they have good eye contact? 11.) How is stride, uniform, headdress and footwear?

A drop is one point deduction, a break or a slip is a two point loss. Baton twirlers are judged on everything from their head to their toes — nothing is left out.

Included in this competition is the Percussion Group or the Drum Corp. This group is judged on their drumming in unison, timing, tuning, interpretation of the music, technique, position, music selections and rhythm. They are also judged on marching and maneuvering, showmanship, entrance and exit appearance, uniform and equipment.

The Percussion Group usually consists of five or six people. They wear a uniform that coordinates with the twirling unit and are led by a baton twirler who gives commands either by voice or by whistle.

NATIONAL COMPETITION

At the national level, the contest is run in much the same way as at the state or local level. The only difference is the greater number of participants and categories.

As many as 5,000 entries have turned out at the national level. And because of the number, more time is needed. A weekend is not enough time for 5,000 competitors to perform, so these meets usually run six days to a week.

Again, a small entrance fee is charged to cover expenses. Most of the time, judges donate their time or are given a small sum to cover their expenses.

Age divisions are much the same, starting with the peewees or preschoolers to the novices (6-8 years old), followed by the juveniles (9-11 years old), then the juniors (12-14), and the seniors (15 and up). Although most of the 5,000 contestants are girls, there are still many boys competing at this level. They have a division all their own.

Time for performers vary from a minute-and-a-half to two-and-a-half minutes depending on the experinece of the twirler. For show routines, they run as long as five minutes. Time is closely watched here to keep on a schedule since so many are waiting to participate.

Different categories and time are:

Baton solo ... time limit 2½ minutes

Two Batons ... time limit 1½ minutes

Pairs ... time limit 2½ minutes

Teams ... time limit 2½ minutes

Strut ... time limit 1 minute

Baton novelty (standard baton used in acrobatics, dance etc.) ... time limit 2 minutes

Novelty baton (hoop, ribbon, fire baton) ... time limit 2½ minutes

Show routine corps of five ... time limit 2½ minutes

Flag swinging ... time limit 2½ minutes

The nationals are judged on a ten point system. Five points for content, variety and difficulty of the routines, another five points for execution, smoothness and showmanship.

State and naitonal baton twirling contests are not the only competitions in the United States. Small towns hold their own contests and often make up their own rules and categories. You might even start your own contest in your neighborhood.

LOCAL ACTIVITIES

High schools and some junior high schools also have added baton twirlers to their band activities. These girls and boys perform during half-time shows at football games and lead the band on and off the field. Baton twirlers or drum majorettes are part of the band unit and add their own color and sparkle to the marching band. The number of baton twirlers used is determined by the band director. The position of the majorettes is facing forward about six yards in front of the drum major in most band formations.

Homecoming parades or Fourth of July parades also use the local talent to lead the All-City Band or the Police Band down Main Street. Baton twirlers find a place here as well.

If your school or community does not have a place for a baton twirler, you might talk with the band director and start a group of your own. Sometimes baton twirling is taught at summer camps for cheerleaders and baton twirlers. Once you begin to twirl the metal shaft, you will be surprised how much fun you can have and the number of tricks you can learn.

A jacket patch worn by a majorette says it all, "Happiness is being a majorette."

ABOUT THE AUTHOR

Nancy Robison is the author of 16 books. She enjoys writing as well as participating in active sports such as skiing, swimming and tennis. At one time, she was a baton twirler and still enjoys it today. Ms. Robison is the author of **Hang Gliding,** another in Harvey House's popular "Free-Time Fun" series of books for young readers.

BLAIRSVILLE-SALTSBURG SCHOOL DISTRICT

Date_____ No._____

Payment will be required for books lost or carelessly damaged.

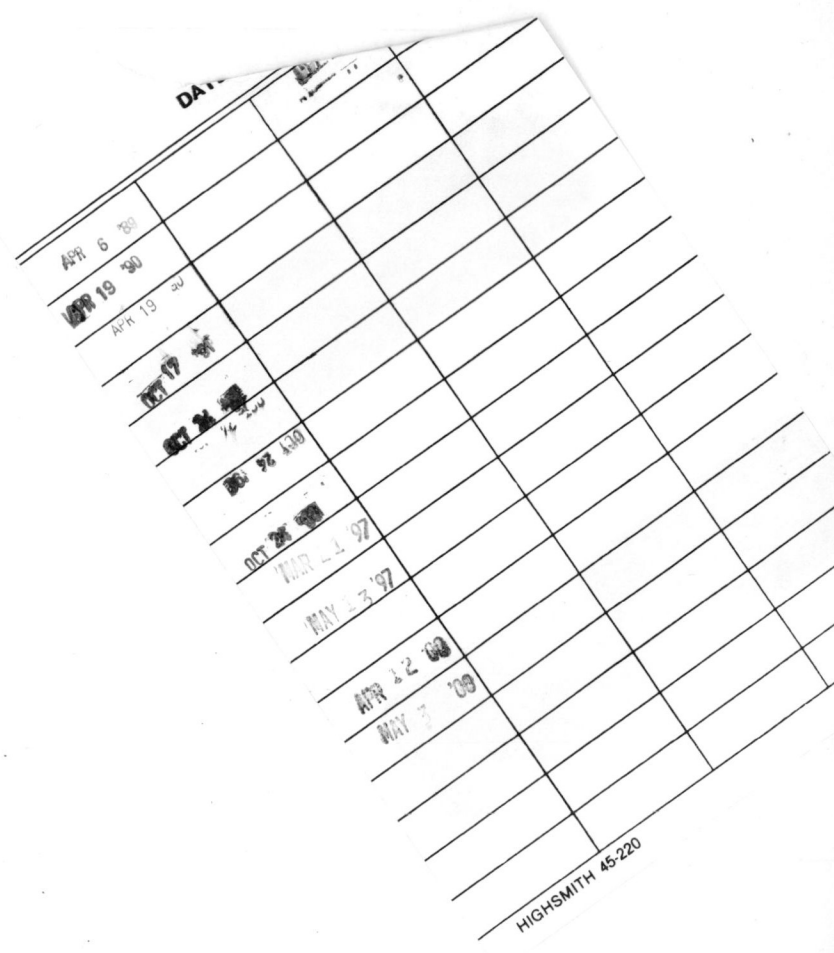